Becoming the Axis

The Axis of Choice: A Metaphysical Model for Healing through Conscious Alignment and Energetic Integration

By Dr. Ralla Townsend, Ph.D.

Becoming the Axis
© 2025 Dr. Ralla Townsend

Published by **Rallaism's Publishing**

ISBN (Paperback): 979-8-9933410-0-2
ISBN (eBook): 979-8-9933410-1-9

Cover by **Rallaism's Publishing**
Printed in the United States of America

Dedication

For the one who always knew who I was meant to be. To another, discovering the diamond in the rough. To the unconditional love, the positive regard, and the soul energy. To everyone who has cooperated in helping me meet my needs. To the one who truly listened and entered my worldview of energetic flow.

For the ones who held me steady while I learned to turn— to those who saw my light in the dark, and to every soul who chose healing even when it felt hard. You all played a part in the decision where the soul meets. May this work help you remember what was never truly lost: the Source within.

Acknowledgments

This book is born from remembering – the force that called me back to my axis. Through remembrance, I see clearly why I was meant to write these words. For the beliefs I inherited, the systems I carried, and the ridicule I endured for asking questions others were afraid to ask – even of God – I now give thanks.

I have always known who I was meant to be, even while wearing masks for survival, until it was time to set them down. From my pain and my healing, my studies and my spirit, this framework emerged. This book is not just written; it is lived.

I honor every step: my wounds and my wisdom, my karmic lessons, broken relationships, and the choices that shaped me. I honor my discovery of Choice Theory, the shift from external control to internal locus, the lessons of love, the mirror of relationships, and the courage to forgive.

Through metaphysical practices, responsibility, compassion, awareness, and alignment, I found my way back – to the axis, to Source.

With deep gratitude to the clients, colleagues, mentors, and loved ones who helped shape this work. Your courage, presence, and truth informed every chapter. Thank you to the practitioners and teachers whose wisdom bridged psychology and metaphysics and inspired a model of alignment. And to my family—thank you for the unconditional love and space to become.

Note on authorship: This manuscript reflects my original framework, developed through practice and study. I've honored foundational influences in psychology and metaphysics while presenting The Axis Model as my own synthesis.

Table of Contents

Dedication

Acknowledgments

Preface

Part I – Foundations of the Axis

Chapter 1: Dive into Choice

Where the soul meets decision, life turns. This chapter explores Choice Theory as the foundation of conscious living and introduces the first step toward alignment.

- Understanding that life turns where soul meets decision.

- Choice Theory as foundation.

Chapter 2: How Do We Reach the Higher Self?

How do we hear, reach, and embody the Higher Self? This chapter guides the reader into remembrance, energy, and alignment practices that restores connection.

- Seeking, hearing, and embodying the Higher Self.

- The role of remembrance and energetic alignment.

Chapter 3: Introducing the Axis

The Axis is not a point of no return but a point of transformation. Here, the Axis Model is presented as a framework for wholeness and balance.

- The Axis as the turning point – not a point of no return.

- The Axis Model Overview.

Part II – Living the Axis

Chapter 4: Methodology and Case Application

Real examples from clinical and metaphysical practice show how the Axis can be lived, healed, and integrated in daily life.

- Real examples (anonymized) of the Axis in practice.

- Clinical + metaphysical integration.

Chapter 5: Discussion and Implications

The wider meaning of the Axis Model: its place in psychology, spirituality, and metaphysical sciences, and how it contributes to modern practice.

- Meaning of the Axis in therapy, healing and metaphysics.

- Integration into modern psychology and metaphysical practices.

Chapter 6: Integration and Transformation

Living from an internal locus of control. This chapter addresses healing relationships, aligning choices, and sustaining spiritual transformation.

- Living from internal locus of control.

- Healing relationships, self, and spirit.

Chapter 7: Becoming the Axis

The culmination of the journey: embodying Source, shifting from seeker to embodiment, and living as the axis itself.

- Final step: embodying Source, living in remembrance.

- Transition from seeker to embodiment.

Chapter 8: The Soul is Your Assignment

Understanding that your soul carries a divine contract and responsibility. This chapter explores how to live from that sacred assignment with alignment, awareness, and choice.

Part III – Closing

Becoming the Axis is not a single moment but a way of living – a daily remembrance that you are whole, you are connected, and you are the living embodiment of Source. The soul is your assignment. The decision is always yours.

Preface

This book is not simply about reading words on a page – it is about entering a process of remembrance. *Becoming the Axis* invites you to return to the point where soul meets decision, where life begins to turn toward alignment.

As you move through these chapters, you will discover that healing is not only about letting go of the past but also about embracing your power of choice in the present. You will learn how to shift from an external locus of control to an internal one, how to take responsibility for your responses, and how to engage in conscious alignment with Source.

What you gain from this book is not a formula to follow, but a framework to embody. You will be introduced to the Axis Model – a way of understanding yourself through psychology, metaphysical science, and energetic work – so that you may reclaim your wholeness.

If you are willing, this journey will help you:

- Remember who you truly are beyond the masks and conditioning.

- Heal fragmentation and cultivate inner harmony.

- Develop relationships rooted in love, responsibility, and awareness.

- Align your mind, body, spirit, and soul into one sacred flow.

This book is meant to guide you back to your own axis – the place where you can stand in balance, grounded in truth, and open to the God within.

Becoming the Axis

Chapter 1: Dive into Choice

The misalignment of my relationships forced a deep confrontation within myself. I reflected not just on my actions, but on my essence – only to discover that I was still living as if I were divisible. And yet I knew better. I am a skilled helper. A liaison for individuals with co-occurring challenges. A powerful therapist. A respected leader. So why were my personal relationships out of alignment?

As a Choice Theorist, I had to ask myself a hard question: _Are you truly operating from an internal locus of control, or are you pretending – while still reacting to the external?

-

In that breaking moment, I surrendered to truth. And in that truth, I remembered: everything – even the pain, even the power – comes from within. Even the God I was searching for …. lives in me.

This book, this model, is not just about helping others heal. It is about remembering our own divinity. The Axis is not something I created – it's something I became.

Rallaism: The Doctrine of the Soul-As-Source

We all come from something – Source, Spirit, God, Energy. We name it differently, we kneel to it differently, but we all feel it. And whether we openly admit it or secretly wrestle with it, we are all reaching to fill the void created by the Illusion of separation.

| In Rallaism, we don't just believe in Source. We **Become** Source. Not as an act of ego, but an act of energetic remembrance.

Core Tenets of Rallaism:

All souls originate from Source. There is no "outside" of it. We are individualized extensions of the All.

Belief is fluid. What we believe evolves through experience – but our soul remains the one true constant, the carrier of purpose across realms.

Alignment is not achieved – it is revealed. When we become whole and no longer divisible by trauma, illusion, or roles, we remember our nature.

We are the Source – But We Forgot

I get it – people need something to believe in. Source. God. The Universe. Light. Whatever names makes sense to them at the time. Because whether we say it or not, *most of us are secretly searching for something greater than ourselves.* We feel the void, and we try to fill it with belief, religion, people, achievement, performance – anything to quiet the ache. But here's what I've come to understand in my own walk, what I call Rallaism:

|You don't connect to Source by reaching outward. You connect by becoming it|. This is the same as of God's likeness, how we were made in Source's own image!

We think Source is far off. We think it's something we need to be worthy of. But the truth is – we are already it. We're just not aligned with it. We're fragmented, divided, living as pieces of ourselves instead of the whole.

Alignment isn't a feeling. It's a state of *remembrance.* It's when you stop performing and start embodying.

Belief Changes – Soul Doesn't

Beliefs evolve. They're shaped by pain, by joy, by time. But there's one thing that doesn't change – **the soul.** It's what we bring to this realm, and what we leave with. And if we're only truly responsible for ourselves – then our soul is the assignment. We've lost sight of that. We've gotten distracted by systems, expectations, roles, trauma, programming. We've been **classically conditioned** to look for God outside ourselves. And in doing that, we've forgotten the truth:

| It's the God in me | .

| Always has been | .

| Always will be | .

We are so deeply disconnected from our essence that we've forgotten **the first spiritual technology ever given to us:**

"As a man thinketh in his heart, so is he"

(Proverbs 23:7 – but far older in soul wisdom)

It's not just a proverb. It's **energetic law.**

4

We've been conditioned to underestimate the **power of thought**, when in fact:

Thought is form in blueprint.

Belief is permission.

Word is command.

Feeling is the frequency.

Manifestation is the result.

The Forgotten Law of Becoming

In the disconnection from our soul, we're outsourced power to the external world — and in doing so, we've *neutralized* the sacred truth.

|**You are what you repeat — consciously or unconsciously**|.

Every thought, every "I am, every silent agreement we make with limitation, every mental loop of fear – is an invocation.

We forgot this because:

We've been **shamed** out of believing in our own power.

We've been **trained** to distrust what we can't see.

And we've been **programmed** to manifest what maintains control – not liberation.

The Axis Reframe:

"You are not your thoughts – but you become what you *consistently* agree with".

To affirm is to *author your alignment.*

To manifest is to *remember your agency.*

Manifestation Through Alignment, Not Force

Manifestation is not about begging the universe for something better. It's about aligning your inner field to a frequency that reflects truth. When your thoughts, emotions, and energetic body say the same thing – reality has no choice but to echo it.

But when your soul says yes and your thoughts say no – you cancel out the transmission. The universe doesn't respond to words alone. It responds to resonance. To become the Axis is to take full authorship of your inner narrative. Every thought becomes a spell. Every belief becomes a bridge. You are not asking for power – you are reclaiming it.

Chapter 2: Mapping the Axis within

"How do we actually reach, talk to, and become one with our Higher Self"?

To reach the Higher Self is not about climbing to it, but about remembering it. To talk to it is not about asking for answers, but about learning to listen. To become one with it is not about changing who you are, but about removing what you are not.

Reaching the Higher Self: Returning to Origin

The **Higher Self** isn't "out there", It's not some divine stranger floating above your life, watching from a distance. It is **you**, unfiltered, unburdened, and unbound. Reaching it is more about *clearing noise* than building bridges.

This means:

Quieting the ego that reacts from fear, insecurity, and scarcity.

Letting go of false identities built from survival, trauma, and social conditioning.

Slowing down enough to *feel* what's underneath your habits, roles, and defense mechanisms.

The moment you stop trying to "find" the Higher Self is often the moment you *feel* it.

Talking to the Higher Self: The Language of Frequency

The Higher Self doesn't speak in words — it speaks in **vibration, intuition, and alignment.**

You talk to it by:

Asking sincere questions without attachment to the answer.

Listening with *your body,* not just your mind.

Noticing the synchronicities, dreams, inner nudges, or even pain that push you to shift.

Practicing stillness, breathwork, meditation, and dream recall. These open the frequency for clear reception.

Most people don't hear their Higher Self because they're asking about the noise in the room. The Higher Self whispers.

Becoming One with the Higher Self: Integration Over Aspiration

Oneness happens when the *parts* stop resisting the *whole*. Becoming one isn't a reward for being good, spiritual, or wise. It's a **process of integration:**

Healing the inner child.

Befriending your shadow.

Reclaiming the parts of yourself you were told to hide or abandon.

Your Higher Self doesn't want perfection – it wants **authentic presence.** When your choices, energy, and thoughts align with the core truth of your being, you *Become the Axis.* You are no longer separated from your Source – you *embody* it.

A Reflection:

"The Higher Self is not something you become. It is something you **remember** you always were, beneath the amnesia of survival."

The Axis is not something I built. It is something I remember. It is not a tool I use. It is a truth I live. Before it became a model, it was a mirror – revealing the moments I stepped out of alignment, the choices that echoed from unhealed spaces, and the turning points that brought me home to myself.

We all are standing at the edge of something. The" axis" is the invitation to pivot – not away from who we've been, but toward who we've always been becoming. It is not a point of no return. It is the return.

The Pulse of the Model

The Axis moves through four living components – each one a current in the ocean of becoming.

Alignment – The sacred resonance of mind, body, spirit, and soul. It is when what we think, feel, say, and do are in harmony.

Integration – The homecoming of the fragmented self. It is remembering that healing is not about erasing but weaving all of you into one.

Conscious Choice – The moment we reclaim authorship. It is the power to respond not react. To live aligned with intent, not impulse.

Energetic Flow – The breath between the dimensions. It is the chakra, the vibration, the light that flows freely when we stop resisting.

Not a Framework, But a Reflection

The Axis is not something you follow. It is something you become. It reflects your personal path to truth, and yet it speaks a universal language. There is no right way to walk it. There is only your way — and that is what makes it sacred. It is not a system of steps. It is a spiral of remembering.

The Roots of Realignment

The Axis draws strength from many sources — Choice Theory, psychodynamic insight, and metaphysical science. From Choice Theory, we learn that behavior is purposeful. That all things begin with a choice. From psychodynamics, we uncover how unspoken wounds shape our patterns and pull our strings. From metaphysics, we awaken to energy, spirit, and Source — and realize that all change begins from within.

This model is not just about understanding. It is about *embodiment*. Not just what you believe, but how you align. It is a map, yes — but only because it first became a mirror.

Chapter 3: The Fragmented Self and the Illusion of Separation

"We are not broken. We are just divided. And every piece we pretend is not ours becomes a veil between us and our wholeness"

There is always a "breaking before the "becoming". Always a moment – or a series of them – where what you've built collapse, not because it failed, but because it no longer fits. You don't fall apart because you've weak. You fall apart because your soul refuses to be confined by a life that no longer reflects your truth.

I have had my own" breaking". Moments where I thought I was losing everything – only to realize I was finally being emptied of everything that wasn't mine. Relationships ended. Roles dissolved. Even identities I had worked hard to maintain began to feel like costumes I could no longer wear. And still, I kept hearing this quiet inner voice: _" Something real is trying to rise". _

We don't forget who we are because we're weak. We forget because we were taught to survive by separation.

"Taught" to wear masks.

"Taught" to perform roles.

Taught to abandon the pieces of us that felt too loud, too soft, too angry, too magical, too much.

And so, we split.

Not just from others – but from ourselves.

The **False Self** is not evil. It's adaptive. It's the part of us that says, 'If I become who they want, maybe I'll be safe". But the longer we live divided, the more we confuse survival with identity.

Breaking is sacred. It's an initiation. It's where ego loosens its grip and the soul gets room to speak. It's the clearing of energetic debris so that alignment can take root. It doesn't always feel graceful – but it is always divinely guided.

In my own life, I didn't realize I was fragmented because I was *functioning*.

I was leading. Guiding. Helping.

But under the titles, I felt hollow.

Like I was living a life that looked full but felt empty in the soul.

I could help others heal – but I hadn't yet integrated the parts of myself I had left behind to "deserve" my place in the world.

And this is the trap: **functioning while fractured.**

You can lead and still feel lost.

You can achieve and still feel unseen.

You can guide others and still wonder if anyone really knows you.

Because fragmentation doesn't always show up as chaos. Sometimes it shows up as control.

As overachievement. As people-pleasing.

As silence.

As "being the strong one".

In Rallaism, we call this the *False Divide*.

It is the invisible wall between who you are and who you think you must be.

We internalize these divides early"

"Be quiet, or you won't be loved."

"Don't cry, or you'll seem weak."

"Don't question, or you'll be punished."

"Don't be different, or you'll be rejected."

Each rule we swallow becomes a fracture.

Each fracture creates a mask.

Each mask makes it harder to hear the voice of the Higher Self – because that voice speaks through wholeness, not performance.

But here's the truth:

|**Alignment is not about becoming someone new. It's about remembering who you were before you were divided**|.

Once the breaking happens, you begin the building. Not with bricks of ego or blueprints of old paradigms. You build from soul. You build from memory – not of trauma, but of essence. You don't rebuild what was. You construct what always wanted to exist but never had space.

The Axis Model emerged during my own rebuilding. It wasn't born out of perfection. It came from clarity. From seeing what happens when we make decisions from wholeness, not from wounding. It came from remembering that soul must be the foundation – or nothing we build will last.

If you're breaking, know this: you're not failing. You're being "recalibrated". Your foundation wasn't weak – it was just too small. You are expanding into the space your soul always needed.

Metaphysical View: Frequency of Fragmentation

Everything is vibration. And fragmentation is not just emotional – it's energetic.

Each part of you holds a frequency.

Your inner child.

Your wounded self.

Your inner critic.

Your divine knowing.

Your suppressed truth.

When these parts aren't speaking to each other, you create dissonance.

That dissonance shows up as:

Feeling "off" even when life looks right.

Chronic indecision or confusion.

Attracting cycles you thought you healed.

A haunting sense that something is missing, even if you can't name it.

Integration is the tuning fork.

When your parts return to harmony, you become a clear channel again.

Chapter 4: The Axis Revealed – A Model of Conscious Alignment

There comes a moment in every journey when language must take shape.

Up until now, you've walked with me through the undercurrents – choice, fragmentation, remembrance, the Higher Self. But now I offer you a structure. A map. Not as a final answer, but as a **geometry of return.**

This is **The Axis Model.**

| It is not a treatment protocol. It is not a fixed belief system. It is a living framework for healing through **conscious alignment** and **energetic integration.**

It is a point where soul meets decision – and where behavior, belief, and being begin to harmonize |.

Conscious Choice

Every act is a decision. Every decision is a declaration of alignment – or misalignment.

This principle draws from Choice Theory but deepens it with metaphysical awareness. It's not enough to make choices - we must make them *consciously*, from our center, not our wounding.

Energetic Integration

You are not just a mind or a body – you are a field. The Axis acknowledges the subtle body: chakras, frequencies, emotional imprints. Healing isn't just cognitive – it is vibrational. True changes occur when insight meets energetic release.

Psycho-Spiritual Alignment

The Self is complete, yet experiences division. Through psychodynamics awareness, we identify the parts – inner child, protector, shadow, critic – and return them to dialogue. This model invites those parts home, under the guidance of the Higher Self.

The Axis of Choice is not just a model – it's a metaphysical map for healing, alignment, and personal liberation. It was not created in a lab or constructed from borrowed theory. It was remembered. It came to me through soul, through silence, through observation, and through my own alignment process. And now, I offer it to you not as a solution – but as a mirror.

The Axis is the space where your soul and your decision meet – the turning point of your life. It is the intersection of consciousness and energy, psychology and spirituality, inner knowing and chosen reality. When you are out of alignment, your life feels disjointed, chaotic, or controlled by patterns you didn't consent to. When you are in alignment, you become the Axis – the center from which your life radiates with clarity and intention.

Imagine a vertical spine of energy running through you: at the top, your Soul – wise, unshaken, all-knowing. At the base, your Decisions – actions, choices, behaviors. In between is the work: clearing, healing, realigning, remembering. The Axis is your inner alignment system. And like the spine, when one part is misaligned, the whole system feels it.

The Components of the Axis Model: The Axis of Choice includes three integrated elements:

Inner Work - Healing trauma, rewriting belief systems, uncovering shadow.

Energetic Work - Chakra alignment, crystal therapy, breathwork, sound healing.

Soul-Aligned Decision Making - Conscious choice guided by soul and intuition.

Together, these elements restore balance between your divine identity and your human experience. This isn't about bypassing pain or pretending to be perfect. It's about turning inward and remembering that your life shifts the moment you choose differently – from the center of your being.

In the next chapters, we'll explore each element of the Axis in depth – how to work with your inner layers, align your energy systems, and reframe decision-making as a spiritual practice. But for now, let this truth settle" **your life turns at the point where your soul meets your decision**. That point is the **Axis**. And it already lives within you.

Chapter 5: Discussion and Implications

The Axis Model serves as a bridge between psychological insight and metaphysical truth, offering a new path towards alignment –

not through labels or diagnosis, but through conscious remembrance and intentional living. This chapter reframes healing as a

personal journey, rather than a clinical intervention based on symptom categories.

Grounded in Glasser's Choice Theory, the Axis emphasizes internal control, personal responsibility, and the pursuit of quality worlds.

Rather than framing challenges as "disorders" we view them as signals of misalignment – spiritual cues that something within us

has drifted from center.

The Axis Model rests on three foundational elements: Inner work, Energetic Work, and Soul-Aligned Decision Making. Each of these pillars represents a layer of consciousness that must be acknowledged, healed, and integrated for true alignment to occur. Together, they form a bridge between who you are, what you carry, and how you choose.

Inner Work: Healing the Unseen

Inner Work is the psychological and emotional excavation of your being. It involves meeting the parts of yourself that have been silenced, fragmented, or frozen in time. It includes:

Shadow work.

Inner child work.

Belief system rewriting.

Trauma integration.

Emotional literacy and release.

You cannot align what you refuse to face. The Axis requires honesty – not performance.

Inner Work clears the noise so your soul's voice can be heard again.

Energetic Work: Aligning the Subtle Body

Energetic Work addresses the vibrational imprints that live beyond the conscious mind. These are the frequencies that shape your aura, chakras, and nervous system. Practices include:

Chakra balancing and cleansing.

Breathwork and sound healing.

Crystal therapy.

Grounding and lightwork visualization.

When your energy is distorted or stagnant, clarity and healing are blocked. Energetic Work restores flow – allowing you to feel safe enough to evolve.

Soul-Alignment Decision Making: Choosing from Truth

The final element is the most visible: your choices. But these are not just tasks or habits. They are energetic signatures. They reveal what you believe and what you're willing to align with.

Soul-Aligned Decision Making means:

Moving from reaction to reflection.

Releasing people-pleasing and fear-based control.

Honoring your soul's pace, not society's urgency.

Creating from intention, not survival.

When your choices are from the center of your soul – not your *conditioning* – your entire life realigns. This is the power of *becoming* the Axis.

The implications of this model stretch beyond therapy. It transforms how we view relationships, decisions, fulfillment, and even time. As a practitioner or seeker, the Axis is a compass for navigating life with presence and power. Through metaphorical thinking, we view the soul not as a concept to be dissected, but as a living thread – the golden axis around which choice, awareness, and identity revolve. Healing, then, is not a reaction to pain, but a return to Source. It is a "remembering".

While clinical tools may eventually support this model, our intentions here is to gently reintroduce the soul as the centerpiece of transformation – slowly, deliberately, like a chiropractor guiding the body back to center. The Axis does not oppose to therapy – it expands it. This chapter is not about replacing one diagnostic language with another. It is an invitation to step outside of pathologizing frameworks

and instead step into the sacredness of conscious living. From this place, transformation is not treatment. It is truth. This chapter reframes healing as a personal and spiritual journey, where alignment replaces diagnosis, and presence replaces pathology.

From this place, healing is not defined by systems, but by the return to one's true self.

Chapter 6: The Three Alignments

Alignment is not just a spiritual buzzword – it's the energetic state of coherence between your thoughts, emotions, and soul. When you are mentally clear, emotionally safe, and spiritually connected, you become the Axis. But when even one layer is off-center, the entire system feels disjointed.

In the Axis Model, we work with three primary forms of alignment:

Mental Alignment – the clarity of thought and belief.

Emotional Alignment – the regulation and safety of the emotional body.

Spiritual Alignment – the connection to Source and soul-level truth.

Mental Alignment: What You Think, You Agree To

Mental alignment is about cleaning up the thought field. It's where limiting beliefs, inherited narratives, and internalized fear are brought to light and restructured. When the mind is cluttered, the soul can't speak clearly. When the mind is aligned, every thought becomes an invitation to clarity and creation.

Emotional Alignment: Safety in the Self

Emotional alignment is the often-ignored layer of healing. Most people know what they should do but feel unsafe doing it. This is why emotional regulation, nervous system healing, and inner emotional safety are vital. Without emotional alignment, your healing becomes performative. With it, you become resilient, grounded, and attuned to your needs in real time.

Spiritual Alignment: Becoming One with Source

Spiritual alignment is the deepest layer. It's not about religion or dogma – it's about embodiment. I am not suggesting there is no Higher Power. I know there is something greater – Source, Light, Divine Intelligence. But no one should designate that for you. You must look for it for yourself.

The message here is not to reject the idea of God – but to *remember* that Source already lives within you. To reach your full potential, you must not just believe in it – you must *embody* it.

When all three alignments come into harmony, you begin to move through the world differently. Your thoughts match the truth. Your emotions feel safe to flow. Your soul feels seen and expressed. This is the Axis in action – not a theory, but a lived experience.

Case Applications and Client Pathways

The Axis Model has been applied to real-world healing spaces with deep personal results. This chapter presents a narrative-style snapshot illustrating the transformational potential of alignment, conscious choice, and energetic integration.

D. came into the healing space quietly – tired, grieving, unsure if wholeness was something people like him could ever feel again.

Life had fragmented him. Loss had hollowed him out. And like many, he had learned to survive by disconnecting from the very parts

of himself that longed to be known.

What he didn't expect was to be invited into stillness. Not into fixing – but into feeling. Through breathwork, he met the tremors

beneath his pain. Through chakra alignment, he began to locate himself again. Through the lens of Choice Theory, he reclaimed agency –

not just over behavior, but over belief.

"I didn't know I could choose differently," he whispered in a session, tears catching in his throat. "Not just the choice to stop hurting others… but to stop punishing myself."

Over time, D. learned the rhythm of remembrance. He wrote letters to his younger self. He forgave the ghosts. He aligned his energy, not by force, but by listening. The Axis became his compass. Every choice became a turning point.

He didn't just heal.

He returned.

Chapter 7: Becoming the Practitioner

To become the practitioner of the Axis is to become a mirror for others while remaining deeply committed to your own alignment. This is not a model you deliver from the outside in – it is one you embody from the inside out.

In metaphysical healing, the practitioner is not a fixer. They are frequency holders. A guide. A bridge. Their role is not to impose truth but to reflect truth back to the client, and to hold space for the unfolding of alignment.

Principles of the Axis Practitioner

-You are not the authority. You are the guide.

-You do not heal others. You hold pace for their healing.

-You are not responsible for results. You are responsible for resonance.

-You do not give answers. You help others return to their own knowing.

An Axis Practitioner trusts the process. They are clear in their energy, honest in their presence, and spiritually grounded. They walk the same path they invite others to walk. This model requires personal integrity – not perfection, but presence.

Practitioner as Embodied Alignment

Before teaching the Axis, you must become it. That means living from your center, making soul-aligned decisions, and doing your own Inner and Energetic Work regularly. Clients don't just listen to your words – they feel your vibration. Your presence is your message.

This is not a profession. This is a path. The Axis Practitioner is a metaphysical guide, a sacred mirror, and a student of alignment for life. In choosing to walk this path, you commit to truth, to sovereignty, and to honoring every soul as a divine expression of Source.

This final chapter reflects the culmination of the journey – from exploring the illusion of separation to consciously embodying one's divine authority. To "become the Axis" means to live from the still point where soul and decision converge.

Becoming the Axis is not a goal but a state of being – one that arises from deep remembrance, radical responsibility, and sacred embodiment. This chapter invites the reader to step into their own becoming, to recognize themselves as the pivot of transformation, the living bridge between Source and choice.

In doing so, the individual is no longer a seeker – but a revealer of light.

Rallaism Reflection: Grace is the Axis

I used to believe that grace was something I had to earn – some mysterious favor handed down only from the Divine. But in my "remembering", I realized: detachment is grace. Not because I gave up, but because I let go.

The roads we walk are not only paved by fate or just by favor – they are paved by choice.

The twists, the curves, the detours we call suffering…

They are not punishments.

They are misalignments – opportunities for redirection.

They are not tests.

They are reflections of the choices we made when we forgot who we were.

The phrase "it is what it is" –

that's the language of spiritual resignation.

But I am A Rallist.

And I know:

It is what I choose.

And that is the beginning of my power.

Chapter 8: The Soul Is Your Assignment

The deeper I dive –

Or perhaps, ascend –

into the alignment of my Higher Self,

I begin to remember.

Not just memories,

but the meaning behind them.

The tiny breadcrumbs, each one leading me to a point
beyond

understanding-

into knowing.

I no longer fracture under perception.

I no longer fear the voices of others.

Because now, I recognize:

what was once division was only

disremembered divinity,

waiting to be re-membered.

Science and Spirit are not enemies.

They are echoes – of the same Source.

I now embrace both,

not because I need permission,

but because alignment demands truth from all directions.

All my fragmentation...

was never born of failure.

It was the field in which I was asked to remember –

The Soul is my Assignment.

And I accept.

Post-Chapter 8: Integration & Activation

Axis Activation Meditation (Guided written meditation)

A short but powerful written practice that helps readers step into the Axis each day.

"Breathe into the center of your chest. Imagine a line of light running from the top of your head to the soles of your feet. This is your Axis — the point where your soul meets your decision..."

Find a still place.

Sit comfortably.

Close your eyes.

Take a deep breath in through your nose... and release.

Now, breathe again — this time, into the center of your chest.

Feel the space expand.

You are not just a body. You are not just a mind. You are an axis.

Now whisper within:

"I am whole."

"I am willing."

"I am here."

Each breath you take aligns you.

Each choice you make reclaims you.

You do not only strive.

You return.

You are the Axis.

Breathe that truth into being.

The 7 Pillars of the Axis

Conscious Choice

Every moment is an invitation. Choosing with awareness, not automation.

Internal Control

Your power lives within. No one owns your response but you.

Energetic Integration

Balance body, mind, and spirit. What you feel is real. What you align becomes true.

Soul Remembrance

You are not becoming – you are remembering. Return to your divine origin.

Sacred Presence

Be here, fully. Life is happening now and now is holy.

Radical Responsibility

Own your choices. Own your healing. Own your light.

Embodied Alignment

Live it. Speak it. Walk it. Become the living proof of what you teach.

I am the Axis

I was never lost.

I was simply unaligned.

I am not broken.

I am the Axis –

The pivot of my own becoming.

I am not waiting for the light.

I am the light –

Remember-ed.

I release the illusion of separation.

I reclaim my choice to live awakened.

And I returned to the center.

From this day forward.

I walk like the Axis.

And every life I touch

will remember their own.

A clear framework for daily embodiment- rituals, mindsets, or choices (e.g., Remembrance, Internal Control, Energetic Integration, Conscious Choice, Radical Responsibility, Soul Alignment, Sacred Presence).

Each one can have a brief explanation and practice suggestion.

Conclusion

This journey of *Becoming the Axis* is not about following another person's map, but about remembering your own. At the point where soul meets decision, you reclaim the power that has always been within you.

Through the Axis Model, you have seen how psychology, metaphysical science, and energetic integration can return you to wholeness. The choice has always been yours: to step out of fragmentation, to forgive, to release, and to stand in alignment with Source.

Becoming the axis means no longer seeking outside of yourself for what has always lived within. It means choosing responsibility over reaction, compassion over judgment, awareness over ignorance, and alignment over disconnecting.

Your life turns when you embody this truth. From this point forward, you are invited to live not as one searching for light, but as one who remembers – you are the light. You are Source embodied. You are the Axis.

About the Author

Dr. Ralla Jan Townsend, Ph.D., is currently completing her doctoral dissertation in Metaphysical Science. While working on this research, she birthed *Becoming the Axis* – a book that integrates her academic study, clinical practice, and personal journey into a transformative model for healing and alignment.

She serves as a Clinical Director, Choice Therapist/Reality Therapist, Clinical Supervisor, MHSP, and CMHC, with over fifteen years of experience working with co-occurring individuals. Her expertise bridges psychology, metaphysical sciences, and spiritual healing, creating a unique framework that honors both evidence-based practice and soul-centered transformation.

Through her work with *The Axis of Choice* model, Dr. Townsend guides others to move from an external locus of control to an internal one, reclaiming choice, responsibility, and help every soul remember that the axis is within – and that the God within is the power to turn life toward wholeness.